GOD DWELLS IN ME

Living in the Power of Your Baptism

JOEL STEPANEK

Published by The Word Among Us Press
7115 Guilford Drive, Suite 100
Frederick, Maryland 21704

26 25 24 23 22   2 3 4 5 6

ISBN: 978-1-59325-590-9
eISBN: 978-1-59325-399-8

Nihil Obstat: The Reverend Michael Morgan, JD, JCL
Censor Librorum
June 24, 2021

Imprimatur: +Most Reverend Felipe J. Estévez, STD
Bishop of St. Augustine
June 24, 2021

Scripture texts used in this work are taken from the *New American Bible, revised edition* © 2010, 1991, 1986, 1970 Confraternity of Christian Doctrine, Washington D.C., and are used by permission of the copyright owner. All rights reserved. No part of the New American Bible may be reproduced in any form without permission in writing from the copyright owner.

Excerpts from the English translation of the *Catechism of the Catholic Church* for the United States of America, Second Edition, copyright © 1997, United States Catholic Conference—Libreria Editrice Vaticana. Used with permission.

Cover design by Suzanne Earl

Made and printed in the United States of America

Library of Congress Control Number: 2021915321

CONTENTS

FOREWORD

By Mark Hart

My parents were great gift givers. At age ten, I got my first skateboard and spent the summer mastering the half-pipe, with no visible skin left on my knees or elbows—and I did not care. At age thirteen, I received a new bike, one that offered me not only a social life—with the ability to connect with friends in distant neighborhoods—but also the chance for a paper route and some financial freedom. At age sixteen, I received a ticket to see my favorite college football team play for a national championship—and win it. It was one of the happiest days of my life.

We all have gift memories that can bring a smile to our faces or warmth to our hearts. For those of us born and raised Catholic, however, it's a moment that we often don't remember—one we too often *overlook*—that offers our greatest and most meaningful gift.

What day were you baptized? Do you know?

Many of us don't know the specific date that we became God's children by virtue of the sacrament, but shouldn't we?

"

At our Baptism,
the Lord said that
we are not merely
his "creation" but
his *child*.

If Baptism really is what the Church says it is and does what Jesus says it does, shouldn't that day stand out above all others on our yearly calendar? Shouldn't Baptism rise in importance over even our birthday or anniversary?

Think about it. At our Baptism, we moved from death to life. At our Baptism, the Lord said that we are not merely his "creation" but his *child*.

Many of us don't think about our Baptism because we don't truly understand the depth and breadth of what happened at it. Most of you reading this were no doubt baptized as babies and have no recollection of the solemn event. Many of us too had parents who dutifully and joyfully had us baptized though they didn't quite understand the theological or ethereal significance of the act. That's not to condemn anyone. At least they saw the importance of Baptism and ensured that we were initiated into Christ and his Church—and we ought to be supremely grateful for that!

This is not to make us sound myopic or thoughtless but to reveal that, when it comes to Baptism, we don't usually view it as possibly the greatest gift our parents ever gave us. Far better than a toy that will break or a bike that will rust or a game that will end, our Baptism is eternal—an unbreakable bond between God and us.

The Church does her best to remind us of its importance. We begin and end every prayer with the Sign of the Cross, reminding us that we were baptized into the familial and covenantal love of the Holy Trinity. In every church, we are encouraged to enter and bless ourselves with holy water, another example and reminder of our Baptism and our escape from death through the waters of new life. During the Easter season, we renew our baptismal promises.

Our Creed reiterates our belief in the Father almighty, affirming our spiritual adoption and childhood in Christ. We light candles, we utter prayers, we have our sins remitted—all in an effort to hearken us back to the most important event in our lives on earth, that moment when heaven declared its presence within us.

Yet most of our hands—in the busyness of the day or stress of the year—hit the holy water font in our local parish and make the Sign of the Cross without a second thought to the cosmic significance of the action.

That's why this little booklet you are holding is such a treasure. The pages that follow offer you an indispensable gift. The author is going to walk you through just what makes your Baptism so life altering. Joel offers some practical ideas on how you can live out your Baptism, live the abundant life that it offers you to its full. With tangible examples and simple yet profound truths, he will give you a new outlook on an ancient ritual. In short, here you will find an invitation to a new life, one steeped in the life God imbued as the water hit your head and as the candle was sparked.

Jesus called us to an abundant life (see John 10:10). We were created by Love for love. We were made to be truly living, not merely breathing.

I invite you now to take a deep breath and exhale. Invite the Holy Spirit to dwell in you anew. Give the Spirit permission to enrapture and enliven your soul and to burn even more brightly in your life and world. Ask the Holy Spirit to be with you and remain in you for eternity.

Understanding your Baptism more deeply will have ripple effects throughout your life. The journey begins with the turn of the page.

Welcome to (new) life!

Chapter 1

A JOURNEY TO ABUNDANT LIFE

I sat in the seat and took a deep breath. I took a look out the window as the plane started to move, picked up speed, and then picked up altitude. Trees, houses, and the small regional airport became more distant, and the clouds moved close. I was flying, and a wave of excitement passed over me. I felt alive.

Have you ever had a moment when you felt exceptionally alive? When everything seemed to be working? Sometimes we have these "life" moments in small ways: We get into a flow at work and seem to be working at a superhuman pace. We round the last turn of a race and think about all the training that brought us to this moment. We witness our favorite sports team winning the championship. We feel alive.

Then there are the big moments—the moments that are life changing—like graduating from college, meeting your spouse, reuniting with an old friend, holding your child for the first time, watching that child graduate from high school. There

"

When we are
baptized, something
spiritual happens
that is irreversible.

is a lot of life in those moments; we might even say there is *abundant life* there.

Flying was an experience of abundant life for me. No one else in my family had ever flown. Yet there I was, at sixteen, flying by myself to a conference. I felt grown up, blessed, and excited.

I forgot about that flight until years later, when I found the ticket as I was cleaning out some boxes from my parents' basement. I sat down and looked at it, allowing the memories to flood back. I saw them with the added memories of later flights I would take.

Sometimes we have opportunities like that—to unpack big moments from our past and see them in a new way. This book is one of those opportunities. This book is about a big moment that we sometimes forget until something else reminds us of it, and even then, we often move right past it without unpacking all that has happened since that moment.

For Christians there is a single moment that changes our world and offers us abundant life, but many of us don't think about it on a daily, weekly, or even monthly basis. We may remember it at a certain time of year—say, Easter—but often it feels more like a piece of history than a cherished moment. That moment is our Baptism, and the life we were given in that moment is called grace.

When we are baptized, our life changes forever. It is a moment that we can't take back and can't erase. Something spiritual occurs that is irreversible. Baptism has not just a symbolic meaning but eternal implications.

Many of us Catholics were baptized as infants. If you are like me, you may need one of your parents or godparents to remind you of the exact date you were baptized. Some of you may have a more vivid memory of your Baptism; maybe you were baptized as a child as your family entered the Church or as an older adult who made the decision after prayer and reflection. Some of you may be preparing to receive the Sacrament of Baptism, excitedly looking forward to that day and what it will mean.

These reflections are for all of us—whether or not we've been baptized. They are meant to help us unpack the powerful moment of Baptism and what it means for us.

MORE THAN A FAMILY TRADITION

Before we dive in (or take off), there are some foundational pieces of Baptism that are worthy of reflection.

The Sacrament of Baptism is not just a symbol or an empty ritual or a kind of "family tradition" we take part in to honor a newborn baby or to welcome new members to a club. The Sacrament of Baptism is a spiritual sign, or symbol, *that brings about what it represents.*

Baptism represents a death to sin and a rebirth to new life. The signs and symbols of that action are the water of a baptismal font, the pouring of water on the head or full immersion into the water, the recitation of the formula of Baptism, and the giving of a white garment and candle to the newly baptized. All of these pieces are visible movements that demonstrate the invisible reality of what is happening in Baptism: the person being baptized is dying to sin and rising with Christ as a new creation. The water, words, white clothing, and lit candle all help us see what is happening. Remember, a sacrament is an outward sign of God's invisible power and grace.

The immersion in water represents our death—the death to sin and the unique way we share in Jesus' death (see *Catechism*, 1227; Romans 6:3-4; cf. Colossians 2:12). In Baptism we rise out of the water, symbolizing Christ's resurrection and what will be our resurrection to eternal life. We are baptized in a specific way—in the name of the Father, and of the Son, and of the Holy Spirit—welcoming us into the love of God and following the formula that Jesus Christ gave to his disciples (see Matthew 28:19). We are given a white garment as a sign of our freedom from sin and a lit candle to represent the light of Christ present within us (see *Catechism*, 1243).

The symbols of Baptism point to a life-changing moment—to a moment of *abundant* life. Baptism purifies us, removes sin from our lives, and makes us whole, holy people.

How do we know all this? It is not only what Jesus taught but also what Jesus did. Jesus himself was baptized, but not for the reasons we are baptized. When Jesus went to the Jordan River to be baptized by his cousin John the Baptist, John initially refused (see Matthew 3:13-17). When John was baptizing, he offered it as a sign of a person repenting of their sin. This was a great gesture, but it did not have any spiritual significance. Jesus did not need this baptism since he had no sin to repent of.

Jesus took the act of baptism and elevated it. In response to John's initial refusal to baptize him, Jesus replied that the action needed to be done to "fulfill all righteousness" (Matthew 3:15). In essence, he was about to make what John was doing even bigger. When Jesus entered the water, the act of Baptism was made holy. A voice revealed that he was the beloved Son of God, and the Holy Spirit was seen descending upon him.

The same thing happens at our Baptism. We too are chosen and given our identity as God's children. We become adopted sons and daughters of God. Not only that, but we are brought into the family of the Church and made sharers in Christ, and we also become part of the mission of Jesus and the Church.

A lot happens in that water, which has a profound impact on our lives forever. We are made dead to sin and risen to life, we become children of God, we are united with Christ, we enter the Church, and we ultimately enter into eternal life in heaven. Together let us reflect on this moment, in order to unleash all the power within it.

So buckle your seatbelt, make sure your tray table is in the upright and locked position, and get ready for the view. We are about to take off.

Reflection Questions

- When have you felt "abundant life" or especially alive? Describe those moments.

- Have you ever reflected on a single moment, perhaps seemingly small, and realized the bigger effect it had on your life? What was it, and what was the impact?

- Were you baptized as an adult or infant? If an adult, what do you remember? If an infant, what have you been told about the day?

Challenge

This week do some research about your Baptism. Where were you baptized? Who was there? Who was the priest or deacon who baptized you? Who are your godparents? Find pictures and listen to stories from that day.

If you were recently baptized through the Rite of Christian Initiation (RCIA), go back to that day, and write down what you remember. Follow up with members of your RCIA class. What do they remember from that day?

Prayer

Father, thank you for offering me abundant life through Baptism and your Son, Jesus Christ. Pour the Holy Spirit on me in a new way, that I may be present to the beauty of my life, even in the midst of routine and challenges. Amen.

Chapter 2

FREE TO LIVE

I apologized over and over, but it didn't matter. My friend was riding away on his bicycle, and I was left standing alone in the middle of the road. I had accidentally run into him as we were riding because I wasn't paying attention, and we both fell off our bikes. He got the worse of the fall.

I got up to check on him and apologize, but he sat on the ground and wouldn't look at me. His face was bright red, and he was breathing heavily. I looked down to where his eyes were fixed and saw it—he had ripped a hole in his new pants. Not only that, but he was bleeding onto the new pants. He was upset, and I just kept apologizing.

"This is your fault" were his only words as he got on his bike. "Don't follow me. I don't want to talk to you, ever." And he rode away.

Being in seventh grade is hard when your best friend says he never wants to talk to you again. I kept saying I was sorry, louder and louder, as he got farther and farther away. It was useless. He was gone.

I felt as if nothing I could do would ever make him forgive me, and as I reflect on the moment, he never did. We started talking again a few days later and moved on, but that break in our relationship (as trivial as it sounds now as an adult) remained.

I have since had many moments like that. Through college and into my adult years, relationships have become strained or even ended because of hurt inflicted by one person on another. Sometimes that hurt was intentional and necessary, as in breaking off dating relationships. Sometimes the hurt was intentional but unnecessary—speaking words that caused deep wounds in a moment of anger or allowing gossip to violate the trust of a good friend. Other times I hurt people or was hurt when that wasn't the intention at all, but still I bore the wound.

I hate being the one who causes fights, and I struggle when people are mad at me. When my wife and I have a disagreement or argument, I immediately want to reconcile and work it out. She, on the other hand, needs to walk away and collect herself. Her way of handling arguments in our marriage is better, and I know that; she is able to step back and collect herself so that she doesn't say anything out of anger or frustration (and so that I don't either).

But I hate the in-between. I don't like the space between "I'm sorry" and "I forgive you." It feels like eternity, and sometimes I feel as if I'll never be forgiven. I fear I'll be standing in the middle of the road by my bike, alone. Sometimes I even worry that God is going to leave me in the middle of the road.

"

Baptism actually removes our sin and restores our relationship with God to what God desires it to be.

OUR REMEDY FOR SIN

In the Church, when we talk about sin, we are talking about relationships. Specifically, we are talking about any action that hurts, weakens, or even destroys our relationships with God and with other people. Sin doesn't just hurt other people; it hurts us. It leaves a wound that festers and can eventually kill us spiritually.

Baptism is the remedy for sin—for what is wounded in all of us. It brings the forgiveness we desperately need.

The Sacrament of Baptism begins with the Sign of the Cross. This sign actually happens a couple of times during the Rite of Baptism, and if we are used to it, we can make it as a matter of routine rather than with reflection. The cross is a symbol and sign of our salvation. When we look at a crucifix or make the Sign of the Cross, we recall something powerful about God's love and forgiveness and his desire for us. The cross signifies the grace of Christ's redemption that was won for us.

Sometimes I find myself waiting for God to forgive me because I think that I am unforgivable. The cross contradicts that. St. Paul, one of the first followers of Jesus and the author of many of the letters we read in the New Testament, wrote to a group of people in Rome, "God proves his love for us in that while we were still sinners Christ died for us" (Romans 5:8).

We didn't do anything to deserve forgiveness. We didn't even apologize, yet Jesus made the move of forgiving us in his death and resurrection. Jesus knows our sins and chooses to forgive them through his death on a cross, and through that death, he opens up the path to eternal life for us.

Baptism is a critical step on that path. The beauty is that we don't do anything to deserve forgiveness and new life; we just accept it. If you were baptized as an infant or if you witness an infant being baptized, this profound reality is on display. A child cannot say they are sorry; in fact, a child has no personal sin to be sorry for.

Our human condition, though, puts a burden on all of us. We are all capable of sin; in fact, we have a tendency toward it. The Church calls this tendency "concupiscence" (see *Catechism,* 1264). It doesn't mean that we will sin, but it does mean that sin will always pull on us. Concupiscence comes from another human condition: original sin. When we talk about original sin, we are talking about the stain and effect of the first sin of our first human parents.

The story of this sin is written in an ancient book of the Bible, Genesis, which talks about our beginning in a poetic and true way. Two people named Adam and Eve chose to disobey God's law, hurting their relationship with God. Because they had a unique relationship with God, their sin has far-reaching consequences for every human—consequences that we can't overcome by our own power.

We can apologize and apologize and apologize, but nothing we do can make God forgive us. We can't earn his forgiveness. I couldn't even earn my friend's forgiveness. I could have bought him new pants (if I had had a job to make money to actually buy new pants), but that wouldn't have necessarily made him forgive me.

So how do we seek forgiveness from God, who is perfect and in need of nothing? Thank God that he makes the first move. Baptism actually removes our sin and restores our relationship with God to what God desires it to be.

Even an infant bears the mark of original sin; Baptism erases that. If a person is baptized as an adult, Baptism removes all personal sin—sins that the person has actually committed—as well. We "die" to sin in Baptism and rise with Christ. We become new.

This doesn't mean that we won't sin again; we probably will. That is why remembering our Baptism is so critical. We remember that God loves us and forgives us. We remember that God makes the first move in forgiving us, even when we can't make the move ourselves. We also remember that sin is going to stop us from entering into that relationship with God, so we desire to continually be "dead to sin" and truly alive (Romans 6:11).

EMBRACING OUR BAPTISMAL PROMISES

In the baptismal rite, we explicitly reject sin in several different ways. It is worth reflecting on this piece when we are tempted or when we do fall into sin. In this part of the rite, called the "baptismal promises," we renounce sin and the spiritual being that tempts us to sin. We then profess what we believe about God and who God is.

The renunciation of sin has the potential to unleash grace in our lives daily. We renew our baptismal promises every year at the Easter liturgy. But we can, and should, remember them often.

The first part of the baptismal promises includes these questions of renunciation. The priest or deacon asks them of those being baptized or of the parents and godparents of the child being baptized:

- Do you renounce sin, so as to live in the freedom of the children of God?

- Do you renounce the lure of evil, so that sin may have no mastery over you?

- Do you renounce Satan, the author and prince of sin?

The person being baptized—or the parents and godparents of the child being baptized—responds, "I do," to each question. But this isn't a onetime "I do." It is a daily one!

Sin can seem glamorous or attractive. Sin can seem to be what will solve our problems or make us happy. But it isn't. It makes us slaves and becomes our master.

Jesus Christ, through the cross, liberated us from needing to be slaves to sin. But we always have a choice. Even after Baptism, we have a choice.

We can choose to reject sin and embrace the freedom that was given to us at Baptism. When we fall to sin, we can remember that we are still offered forgiveness; we only need to ask. We can go to another sacrament, the Sacrament of Reconciliation, and be healed from our sin so we can start anew. We can go back to that moment right after we were baptized, when we were made new. We can promise again to reject sin.

We don't need to stand begging for forgiveness from God; we need to remember our Baptism and the free gift of forgiveness that is waiting for us. We need to be humble enough to move from the middle of the road and ask.

Reflection Questions

- Have you ever been caught between "I'm sorry" and "I forgive you"? How did it feel?

- Do you ever feel as if you need to earn God's forgiveness by doing specific actions or saying specific prayers? Have you ever felt you were still waiting for God to forgive you for something you've apologized for?

- When have you experienced reconciliation in a relationship? How did that feel?

- Where do you see sin portrayed as glamorous? How do those sins make people into slaves? Have you ever experienced a movement from the "glamour of sin" to "slavery to sin"?

Challenge

Sometime in the next two weeks, make an examination of conscience, and receive the Sacrament of Reconciliation. As you do, remember that this sacrament is not meant to shame us or make us feel guilty. It is a sacrament of mercy that brings peace to our hearts when we are troubled by sin. There is also real grace that comes with the sacrament, and this grace empowers us to turn from sin and live in freedom.

Prayer

Lord Jesus Christ, through your death and resurrection, you gained for me the promise of eternal life. Please send the Holy Spirit to help me see the places where I have refused your gift, so that I can turn from them and experience the abundance of life you promise. Amen.

Chapter 3

ADOPTED AND NAMED

Nothing my son or daughter does will ever make me love him or her less.

It is odd to write a sentence that says so much when my children are both still young. There is a lot of life to live and a lot that they could do to disappoint me, reject me, or hurt me. There are a lot of actions they are capable of committing that could very reasonably make me dislike them or even want to disown them.

Yet I feel confident writing that sentence, and I feel confident speaking those words to them. I can't describe why I know that nothing they do will ever make me love them less, but I know that the statement is true. I'm not perfect, but I strive to be a good father.

I think a lot of parents can relate. We are imperfect people, but something in us wants to love with a perfect love. That love that we feel toward our children is not a human love; it has a supernatural component. If we are made in the image and likeness of God, then this love reflects, though in an imperfect way, who God is and how God loves.

There are, unfortunately, parents who do not love their children this way. I have friends who never heard their moms or dads say, "I love you," and that could be true for you too. Parents and family members can cause deep wounds in us. They can also wound our understanding of who God is, especially when we call God "Father" or compare God's love to the love of parents.

The Sacrament of Baptism offers a beautiful medicine for such wounds and a powerful amplification of the love of good parents. Let's go back to one of the lines we reflected on as we discussed our renunciation of sin: *Do you renounce sin, so as to live in the freedom of the children of God?*

"Children of God." There is a lot going on in those words.

When we are baptized, we are not just forgiven of our sins, but we are brought into a family. We are called—chosen—and our relationship with God changes from "creature" and "Creator" to "son" or "daughter" and "Father." There is a deeply personal and intimate connection here.

Bear in mind that God loves all creation, and human beings are a special creation that God loves in a unique and profound way. Every person has a soul that is eternal. Baptism restores our relationship with God to what God intended it to be—as children, not just creations.

How can God take a creation and make it a child? We become God's children through grace. When we say the word "grace" (and we say it often during Mass), we may not really know the bigger reality that we are talking about. As Catholics, our understanding overlaps with a Protestant understanding of grace in some ways but differs in some significant ways.

GRACE: THE POWER THAT TRANSFORMS US

Grace is free and undeserved favor given by God. This definition we share with all Christians. When we speak about grace, we are talking about favor that God gives, that we do not earn or deserve. Nothing we do can make God give us grace. It is a total gift of love.

Grace is what we need for justification. It is what we need in order to stand in a right relationship with God. We need this grace of justification because of our sin.

Grace is more than favor though. It is a sharing in God's divine life. Whereas other Christian denominations might look at grace as a kind of paint that covers us so that we can be acceptable before God, the Catholic Church views grace as something powerful that transforms us from the inside out. Grace is God's life inside of us; how could we not be transformed by that?

The grace we receive in the Sacrament of Baptism is called "sanctifying grace," which is a grace that never leaves us. When we talk about this kind of grace, we even refer to it as the "seed of salvation." This grace makes us children of God. It is through this grace that we are able to call God "Father" in a real, or substantial, way. We are given God's life—grace— and if we continue to nurture it through the sacraments, it will bear fruit in eternal life in heaven, which is why it is the seed of salvation.

"

Grace is God's
life inside of us;
how could we not
be transformed
by that?

We can reject or ignore this grace, but we can never get rid of it. If we die and are denied entry into heaven, it isn't because we lost this grace but because we failed to accept it and nurture it.

Grace changes us, even if we don't feel that change constantly or in substantial ways. Grace is what allows us to believe in God, to hope in God, and to love God. We can't do those things on our own; our sinful nature prevents us from producing that faith, hope, and love. Any act of faith, hope, or love is prompted by grace from God.

Grace gives us the strength to grow in virtue and to make good moral decisions that help us grow in holiness. It helps us live as children of God.

After Baptism, grace helps us continue to grow in our faith, but we can get lost along the way. We can forget our identity as children of God and find ourselves living no longer in freedom but in slavery to sin. This is where grace gives us a jump start: it reminds us of our calling to be children of God.

There are ways we can nourish, strengthen, and unleash this grace. This happens through the other sacraments of the Church, which all build on the grace given at Baptism. Baptism is the gateway to the other sacraments.

GROWING IN OUR GRACE

The Eucharist gives nourishment for our souls and for the sanctifying grace we received at Baptism. When we receive the Sacrament of the Eucharist in a state of grace (that is to say, not in a state of serious sin), it amplifies the sanctifying grace we received at Baptism. We become spiritually stronger and more deeply connected with Jesus.

If we find ourselves in a state of serious sin, the Sacrament of Reconciliation can restore us to a relationship with God so that we can continue to build on the grace we received in Baptism. As with any child who seeks forgiveness from a kind and loving parent, forgiveness from God is always available. Nothing we do can make God love us less, and this is on display within the Sacrament of Reconciliation. Here we are challenged, once again, to renounce sin and live in the freedom of the children of God.

Those two sacraments—the Eucharist and Reconciliation—empower us to live in the freedom we have as children of God. This freedom is abundant life.

If grace is God's life, then it is *abundant life*. It is life that overflows from us, as we protect it and allow it to grow. This abundant life produces joy and peace—the kind of joy and peace that can only come from knowing we are loved by a God who is not simply some distant Creator but a close and intimate Father. This Father loves us in a way we can glimpse in the best parents in this world, and yet even the most perfect human parent's love comes nowhere near the love that God offers.

And nothing you do could ever make God love you less. You are his beloved son or beloved daughter. He is pleased with you.

Reflection Questions

- What are your family relationships like? Where do you see God's love reflected in those relationships? Where is it challenging to see that love?

- Where in your life have you experienced grace (God's divine favor and help)? Have you ever had an experience of grace that you "felt"? Describe the moment.

- In addition to receiving the Sacraments of the Eucharist and Reconciliation, what else can you do to strengthen the grace you received (or will receive) at Baptism?

Challenge

This week make two commitments. The first commitment is to attend a Eucharistic experience outside of Sunday Mass and to use that moment to simply be with Jesus without expectation. This could be a time of Eucharistic Adoration or a daily Mass.

The second commitment is to write a short note or letter to someone you love and express your love and appreciation for them. A parent, your spouse, or one of your children are possible recipients.

Prayer

Jesus, thank you for the gift of grace that you offer so freely to us in the sacraments. Open my heart to receive that grace more fully when I receive the Eucharist. Do not permit me to put up obstacles that would hinder the good work you wish to do in my life. I ask this in your name. Amen.

Chapter 4

SPEAK, PRAY, SERVE

Jesus is our Savior. He is the full revelation of God. Jesus is the face of God revealed to us. Jesus shows us who God is. And Jesus also shows us who we are.

When we look at Jesus, we not only learn something about God, but we experience a revelation about who we are. Baptism doesn't just make us members of God's family; it makes us members of Christ. It grafts us into who Jesus is. And when we lean into that membership, we discover who we are called to be.

There are three intentional and specific "offices" that Jesus fulfilled perfectly. All three were important offices for the Israelite people and within the history of God's relationship with humanity. Jesus was the perfect prophet, priest, and king.

PROPHETS, PRIESTS, AND KINGS

The word "prophet," when translated from the Hebrew language, literally means "God's mouthpiece." A prophet speaks on behalf of God. Throughout history there have been many prophets. The Old Testament contains the words and actions of many of these; there were also many prophetic voices that are not recorded. There were even "bad" or "false" prophets—people who claimed to speak on behalf of God but did not (see Jeremiah 29:31-32).

The prophetic office was an important one. Often the prophets called people back to God. Many also foretold the coming of the Messiah, or Savior—Jesus Christ—through whom God would save all humanity.

Priests were important throughout human history as well. A priest mediated the human and the divine realms. Priests are found in all religions; in the Judeo-Christian tradition, they have a special role as mediators between humanity and the one true God. A priest would offer prayer and sacrifice—sacrifice that often consisted of animals but could include other goods. Through sacrifice the priest acknowledged God as the source of all gifts and demonstrated a trust in God, who was and is.

Kings have directed people and been responsible for the well-being of their nation. The kings of Israel had added responsibilities: they needed to direct people toward God; they were responsible for ensuring that both civil and religious laws were followed; and they were to guarantee that any foreign gods, not just foreign invaders, were kept out of the country. Unfortunately, many kings in Israel did not live up to this task but allowed people to stray from God and allowed false gods to enter Israel.

Jesus is the perfect prophet, priest, and king. He is God's perfect revelation, the perfect mediator between humanity and

God, because he is fully human and fully divine. He is the perfect king, the fulfillment of the Law and true ruler of all creation.

Jesus shows us who God is, and he also shows us who we are. When Jesus was baptized, he opened up a sacramental reality that, when we enter into it, unites us as members of Christ. This means that we also become prophets, priests, and kings.

This reality of our identity as prophets, priests, and kings is signified in the Rite of Baptism by an anointing with sacred chrism—a scented oil that represents royalty. (If you've ever been at an infant Baptism, you've probably noticed parents, godparents, and other family members smelling the child's forehead, appreciating the scent of chrism.) When prophets, priests, and kings were anointed, a special oil was used, as a sign of God's favor. We maintain this symbol at Baptism to represent our anointing as prophet, priest, and king.

LIVING IN OUR ANOINTING

The grace we receive in the Sacrament of Baptism, when unleashed, helps us be like Christ in these three areas. When we really live this "triple anointing," we become living representations of Jesus Christ in our world. We share in the royal and prophetic mission of Jesus. How can we exercise these offices more fully?

PROPHETS

As prophets, we can be God's voice in our world. This happens in a variety of ways.

We may think of a prophet as someone who thunders the voice of God. But we see in Scripture that sometimes the voice of God is a soft whisper, and prophets spoke comfort as often as they spoke rebuke (see 1 Kings 19:11-13; Isaiah 40:1). We can be God's voice speaking comfort and peace to friends and neighbors in times of difficulty. We become a prophetic voice when we proclaim the hope we have in Jesus in times of distress or despair. And yes, we lean into our prophetic voice when we rebuke others who are sinning and call them to freedom.

We become prophetic voices when we speak up against injustice, by which others are being hurt. A prophet feels deeply with God; you will know you are leaning into your prophetic office when your heart starts to hurt for the things that make God's heart hurt, especially the concerns of those facing poverty, marginalization, vulnerability, and rejection. A prophet cannot help but speak out against the things that break God's heart, and he cannot help but proclaim the freedom and peace that are found only in Jesus Christ.

Being a prophetic voice in our world requires courage. It is easier to stay quiet—even in moments when we should speak up to comfort others—because we don't want to make anyone upset. We have been conditioned to "mind our own business," and so we let our voices be silent. Being a prophetic voice means speaking up for what God cares about and being courageous in doing so.

Priests

We are also anointed as priests. It is important to note that this priestly role that we are baptized into is different from the sacramental priesthood. When a man is ordained a priest, he receives special grace to act in an office as a priest of Jesus Christ. But every baptized person is part of a "common priesthood of believers," which has an important role in the Church and in our world.

A man ordained to the priesthood offers spiritual sacrifice in a specific way through the sacraments, dedicates his life to Christ and Christ's Church, and lives in the service of Christ and the Church. He mediates the human and the divine realms in a specific way. The common priesthood of believers does this as well, but in a different way.

We are called as a common priesthood to a life of prayer and spiritual sacrifice. We even have a part of the Mass in which we are called to offer up our spiritual sacrifice. It happens at the start of the Liturgy of the Eucharist, when the altar is prepared. The priest says, "Pray, brethren, that my sacrifice and yours may be acceptable to God, the almighty Father."

Did you catch the words "and yours"? As the priest is preparing the altar, we are offering up a spiritual sacrifice on that same altar. We are taking the prayers people have asked us to pray, our joys from the past week, and all of the good things and all the difficult and challenging things, and we are offering them up to Jesus as our spiritual sacrifice. There is power in this moment.

"

Jesus gave the
perfect example
of what being a king
really means when
he washed the feet
of his disciples the
night before he
was crucified.

The Mass isn't the only place where we offer a spiritual sacrifice. In our common priesthood, we are present in the world, bringing the spiritual and divine realities into the ordinary. We work jobs with people from many walks of life and backgrounds. We probably know believers and nonbelievers. We can bring the spiritual reality into our daily realities.

This priestly presence can be powerful. Just as someone may see an ordained priest and recognize in him someone who represents what is divine, our lives can send the same message. By living our faith, we become signs of who Jesus is.

Leaning into this common priesthood means living a life of prayer and service. It means saying we will pray for others—and actually praying for them. It is being a spiritual leader for our friends and families, especially if we are parents. We can invite others to pray with us, lead Bible studies, or simply be persons to whom others can ask questions of faith.

Kings

We are also kings—that is to say, we have a royal dignity. The grace here isn't so much in how we rule over other people but in how we serve them. Jesus gave the perfect example of what being a king really means when he washed the feet of his disciples the night before he was crucified.

Jesus is a king but not a tyrant king. He is a king who serves people, and in doing so, he shows who God is. We are called to imitate his example.

When we think about Jesus washing feet, we might glamorize the reality. We think of perfectly pedicured toes, bleached white bath towels, and a glass basin. The reality is far from that picture. Feet were gross in Jesus' time (and many people still feel they are): people wore sandals, so at the end of the day, feet were muddy, dusty, and covered in whatever was in the street.

One job of a servant was to wash the feet of dinner guests. It was a humble job. Someone of higher rank sat above the servant, who knelt and washed their feet.

Jesus did that. Not only did he wash Peter's and John's feet; he also washed Judas' feet. Judas had not yet left to betray him (see John 13). Jesus washed the feet of someone who was about to be responsible for his death.

Sometimes I stay mad for days at someone who cut me off in traffic. Jesus shows us that being a king means serving others, doing it humbly, and showing love for all, even when we seem to be enemies. We can live out this servant kingship in a variety of ways.

We can first love and serve those closest to us. While this may seem easy, those we love the most can also be the most difficult to serve. We can go above and beyond to serve our spouse by taking on chores or responsibilities that normally he or she has. We can serve our children by stepping away from work to play with them (even when the game is robots vs. aliens vs. princesses, and you aren't sure which one you are supposed to be). We can serve our friends by listening to them—really listening—rather than waiting to talk.

On a bigger scale, we can serve people who are marginalized. I struggle to serve those who are displaced and homeless because it makes me afraid. I don't know how to talk or act. I feel out of place. I feel pity but not empathy—which is why I know working with people who are homeless is good for me. It humbles me, and it is where I end up encountering Christ.

We wash feet when we walk away from the political argument, when we don't give in to the temptation to fight with our enemy, when we choose to let go of the grudge. We wash feet when we love our enemies just by praying for them and, if you are really radical, praying for good things to happen to them (part of that "good" being their conversion, if they are in need of it).

Through our Baptism, we are given a triple anointing as prophet, priest, and king—as God's voice, God's presence, and God's hands as servants. Our world needs us to live in those offices, because the offices don't simply come with titles. They come with power and a mission that can change our world if we allow Christ to work through us.

Reflection Questions

- Where do you feel you could do a better job using your prophetic voice? When has someone been a prophetic voice to you?

- What spiritual sacrifice can you offer this week through your work and your prayer?

- Whom can you serve more intentionally this week, in a humble way?

Challenge

Whose feet do you need to wash? Are there people you need to forgive? Are there people you need to serve? Do you need to spend more quality time serving your family?

Spend some time reflecting on whose feet you need to wash and how you might do this. In the next month, make a commitment to wash their feet. This may mean rearranging your schedule to accommodate volunteering or being present, or it may mean reaching out to reconcile with someone with whom you have a strained relationship.

Prayer

Lord Jesus Christ, you were prophet, priest, and king, and by my Baptism, you extend this anointing to me. Please give me eyes to see the places where I need to serve and the people I need to love in your name. Send the Holy Spirit so that I may have the courage to wash feet and, in doing so, bring glory to God the Father. Amen.

Chapter 5

THE MISSION
AND THE BODY

Running a major event can require a lot of moving pieces. If just one part of the system breaks down, everything can fall apart.

I've been a part of many such productions that were incredibly fun but also presented a lot of challenges. Whether it was a conference, concert, or even a large church service, there was always a lot happening behind the scenes that participants wouldn't see.

If event organizers are doing their job, most people don't think about the details. They see a seamless production that allows them to enter into the moment. The second something goes wrong, though, the illusion is broken.

The only way an event can be what it is intended to be is that everyone do their part.

Many parts, one mission. Many parts, one body. St. Paul talked about the early Church in this way, but he wasn't in the

"

Every person that
has been baptized
brings a new piece
to the body of Christ
and to the mission.

business of event organization. He recognized that the "product" of the gospel wasn't a product at all but a life that people needed to be invited into. He recognized that the movement of Christianity, the Church, needed all kinds of people to do all kinds of things in order to share the incredible news of who Jesus is and what Jesus does in our lives.

When we are baptized, we become part of this mission. We are anointed as prophets, priests, and kings in order to bring Christ into the world. We also bring the uniqueness of who we are to that mission field. Every person who has been baptized brings a new piece to the body of Christ and to the mission.

THE CHURCH AS SACRAMENT

The mission of the Church isn't an optional piece of the Christian life; it is central to our lives. We talked early on about how a sacrament is an outward sign of God's invisible grace; the Church is also a sacrament.

The Church is a sign of God's invisible grace; it is a sign of salvation to all humanity. The Church exists to share the good news, or gospel, of Jesus Christ. The Church exists to point people toward Jesus, who is our Savior, so that all people might be with God one day in a perfect way, in heaven.

This has been the mission of the Church since its beginning. One of the last commands Jesus gave to the disciples was to "go . . . , baptizing . . . in the name of the Father, and of the Son and of the Holy Spirit" (Matthew 28:19). The mission of the Church is to bring people into relationship with Jesus, through Baptism.

Baptism makes us part of that mission to go forth and bring more people in. Baptism is at the center of the Church's work. This doesn't mean we only seek to baptize people and then forget about them. If that were the case, the Church would be content to baptize infants and then leave people alone. The Church exists as a community that supports all members.

When St. Paul wrote about the Church being like a body, he also wrote that this mystical connection brings joy and suffering. When one part suffers, St. Paul wrote, we all suffer (see 1 Corinthians 12:26). When someone in our community is hurting, we all should hurt.

A parish community, as well as the greater Church, weeps when a wife loses her husband to illness and grieves when parents bury a child. We stand in solidarity with the family that has become homeless and the veteran who will wrestle with a disability for the rest of his life. We have an obligation, as baptized members of the community, to walk with each other.

The other side of that coin is that we are people who rejoice with others. We celebrate our community and the good things that happen.

We journey with each other in good times and difficult ones. This is one of the ways that our faith can actually be strengthened. We are baptized into a community, so we don't ever have to walk alone in our journey of life.

SHARE WHAT YOU LOVE

The mission of the Church is lived out, then, in two ways. First, we share Jesus with others. We are ready to answer questions, pray, talk about how Jesus has made a difference in our lives, and invite people to experience that. This is a process we call "accompaniment." It means that we walk with people, always ready to share our faith and invite them in. But that doesn't mean we are forceful. We don't push our faith onto others; we invite them into it.

Are you walking in life right now with people who aren't following Jesus? Those are people Jesus wants to encounter. He can encounter them through you.

The second way we live out the mission of the Church is by leaning into the community of baptized believers, to support them and be supported by them. Our faith cannot grow in isolation; we need the body of Christ, the Church, to help us. We continue to grow in our faith after Baptism, with the help of others.

We can lean into our community by getting more involved at our parish. So often we lean into Sunday Mass but little else. Find places to serve and places to find community outside of Mass.

Maybe that isn't possible given your schedule. If that is the case, find ways to engage more fully in Sunday Mass. Do you know the people who sit around you every week? Introduce yourself. Get to know their stories. Can you grieve with them if they are sad? Would you even know? Can you celebrate their victories and the big moments of their lives?

I encourage you to get to know the people at your parish. Even if you do nothing else, this small action can bear big fruit.

Finally, seek out places for continued growth in your faith. As we learn more about our faith and Jesus, we will become more passionate about sharing them with others.

When I learn something new and exciting, I always tell my wife. Sometimes she is excited too, sometimes she seems annoyed, and sometimes she is indifferent. I still share it with her. Sharing our faith is the same: sometimes people will be excited, sometimes indifferent. Rarely will they be annoyed or angry.

When we care about something, we share it. As we grow in love with Christ and the Church, we want to share them.

Ultimately, the mission of the Church is simple: to help people get to heaven. That's what the sacraments are for. They impart the grace we need, which bears fruit in eternal life. That is a message worth sharing, and we all have a part to play.

Reflection Questions

- Where are you most comfortable sharing your faith? Where are you most uncomfortable?

- How can you engage more actively within your parish community? What can you start doing now?

- How will you move forward in supporting others in your community of faith?

- What will you do to continue to learn and grow in your faith after you finish this book? What is your next step?

Challenge

The Church has a mission, and by our Baptism (and Confirmation), we share in this mission in a unique way. Our combination of gifts and talents can build up the Church and help others know Jesus. Not everyone needs to work for the Church in order to share the message of Jesus Christ.

Spend time reflecting on and drafting a personal faith mission statement. How does your life serve the greater mission of the Church in a unique way?

If you are married, create a statement for your family. What does it look like for your family to live out faith in the mission of the Church? Once you decide on the statement, print it and post it where you and your family can see it daily.

Prayer

Holy Spirit, empower me to live the mission of the Church in sharing the saving message of Jesus Christ. Give me courage and boldness in times when I am afraid, counsel and understanding when I don't know what to say, wisdom and knowledge to speak the truth well, and piety with a reverence and awe of God that allows me to be a model of faith to all whom I meet. Amen.

DESTINATION: ETERNITY

It is a simple moment, with the most fundamental signs: water, oil, words, and a community. Yet what happens in that simple moment transforms a person. For some of us, it happened when we were too young to remember the details, and for others, it is etched firmly in our minds. Some of us are still waiting for the moment.

Baptism changes everything: who we are, where we've been, and where we are headed. If we really want to unleash the grace of Baptism in our lives today, then we need to fix our minds on the destination toward which Baptism directs us.

There was a time when people needed maps to get where they were going. A family car trip always involved a giant paper map of the state (or even the entire country), which the person riding up front in the passenger seat would read. That large map took skill to read, and if things got really bad, it would wind up on the hood of the car at a rest stop with several people peering at it to figure out the next turn. If you misread the map or took a wrong turn, you could go miles out of your way before noticing that something was wrong.

Modern technology and GPS have made almost obsolete the classic scene of a family sitting at a rest stop poring over a map. Any person who owns a phone likely has an app that does "turn by turn" navigation. All we need to do is input the place we want to go (you don't even need an address most of the time), and the system will take us there.

If we cooperate, that is.

I've been with drivers who insist they know better. They assure me they know the shortcut. They are convinced the navigation app is "glitchy" and unreliable. They try to make their own way.

I do it too. I am almost always wrong. I just can't beat that navigator. Not only does it help me avoid traffic that I can't see and accidents I am not aware of, but it also frees my mind to focus on driving safely. I can listen to directions and not look for road signs or have to glance at a map or poorly written directions. If I trust the navigation system, I get where I want to go.

THE GREAT FAMILY REUNION

When we are baptized, we are given the directions to our final destination and the means to get us there. Baptism sets us on a journey toward heaven!

As members of God's family, we are all bound for the greatest family reunion of all time in heaven. That destination is firmly stamped on us: we call it an "indelible mark," and this is our ticket to the great family reunion for eternity. We say that

Baptism is the "seal of eternal life" and that it marks us "for the day of redemption" (*Catechism*, 1274, quoting St. Irenaeus and St. Augustine). We are given the grace we need to find our way, and the Holy Spirit guides us, helping us avoid trouble and find the best route.

But we need to listen.

Our indelible mark doesn't guarantee heaven. We could choose to ignore it. We could shut out the voice of God in our lives. We could decide we know a better way. We could decide to abandon the path.

Baptism doesn't override our free will. While we've been given grace and the promise of heaven, we can reject that by our actions. We can choose to let the grace sit. We can fall off the path. God is always there to draw us back; our God is a God of mercy. We can start listening to directions again and be reconciled to God, so we can hear clearly and get back on the pathway to salvation.

But we are also limited by time. We never know when the journey will be up. Every trip has an end.

One of the sobering pieces of the baptismal rite is when a person is given a white garment and candle. The white garment represents the fact that the person is a new creation and has "put on Christ"; the candle represents the fact that Christ has enlightened the person and made them the "light of the world" (*Catechism*, 1243, quoting Galatians 3:27; Matthew 5:14; cf. Philippians 2:15).

This is a picture-worthy moment, especially for an infant Baptism. The parents, godparents, and family gather around an adorable baby in a baptismal robe, and one of them holds

"

Really, living every day in the hope of heaven and following the grace and promptings of God are what abundant life is all about.

a white candle. The words of the priest or deacon reveal much about these symbols. As the white garment is presented, the priest or deacon says,

You have become a new creation and have clothed yourself in Christ. May this white garment be a sign to you of your Christian dignity. With your family and friends to help you by word and example, **bring it unstained into eternal life.**

And then for the presentation of the candle, which is lit from the Easter candle in the church:

Parents and godparents, this light is entrusted to you to be kept burning brightly so that your children, enlightened by Christ, may walk always as children of the light and, persevering in the faith, **may run to meet the Lord when he comes with all the Saints in the heavenly court.**

Both prayers reference the destination that Baptism gives us—heaven—and they give us two symbols: a white garment and light.

THE HOPE OF HEAVEN

Interestingly, these symbols come up again during the funeral liturgy. At the beginning of that liturgy, the coffin is draped with a white cloth and sprinkled with holy water, reminders of Baptism. The Easter candle is present, a reminder of the light of Christ entrusted to the person being buried. These symbols directly connect back to Baptism: the indelible mark that prepares us for our day of death and entrance into eternal life.

Really, living every day in the hope of heaven and following the grace and promptings of God are what abundant life is all about. It is a journey and an adventure with Christ that allows us to turn from sin so we can be free—free to be part of a community and the family of God and part of a mission in which we engage as prophets, priests, and kings.

Baptism isn't a rite of passage or simply a tradition. It is a life-changing moment. It offers us abundant life today and eternal life with Christ.

The grace is waiting for you to live out today. The grace is there to lead you home. The choice to unleash that grace and step into the adventure and the journey is yours.

Reflection Questions

- Where have you felt God's promptings in your life, his directions for you? Is it easy or difficult for you to follow those promptings? What gets in the way?

- Have you ever been to a funeral liturgy? Where have you seen the signs of Baptism?

- What holds you back from unleashing the grace of Baptism in your life?

Challenge

There are fourteen "works of mercy" that the Church identifies. These works of mercy allow us to serve the bodily and spiritual needs of our brothers and sisters. One of the works of mercy is to bury the dead.

We don't usually seek out funerals, but oftentimes they are open to the public. In the next month, attend a funeral at your parish community, and pray with the family and for the deceased person. Pay attention to the baptismal imagery present in the funeral rite.

Prayer

God the Father, you breathed life into me and made me an adopted child through your Son, Jesus Christ. By the power of the Holy Spirit, may I walk my faith well and one day enter into eternal life with you. Amen.

AFTERWORD

The final draft of the original manuscript for this book was completed and turned into my publisher on March 23, 2020, only a few days after the COVID-19 pandemic took firm hold in the United States. It was a period of time filled with uncertainty and fear. Looking at the final words of the last chapter, I am struck by how they ring true. In the midst of a global pandemic, every person is confronted with the reality of death in a heavy and deep way.

In the midst of this reality, we hold on to a profound hope, as death brings with it the promise of new life in Christ. That is why, perhaps now more than ever, reflecting on the Sacrament of Baptism is crucial for our faith. The beginning of our journey of faith foreshadows the end.

We enter into the water of Baptism to die with Christ, and we rise out of the water of Baptism as we will one day rise. What we do in the middle of that journey is dependent on how we respond to the Holy Spirit, with whom we have a relationship, and lean into the gifts and grace that the Holy Spirit provides.

At your Baptism, you made promises of faith. If you were too young to make those promises on your own, your parents and godparents made them on your behalf. Every year at Easter, we profess these baptismal promises again, renewing our fidelity to them. I believe that the renewal of baptismal promises plays a crucial role in our world today. It is a reminder of what Baptism is for us and who we are to be in a world that needs hope.

The promises begin with a rejection of things that make false promises. Satan, the devil, is a liar. Right after Jesus was baptized, Satan tempted Jesus with false promises (see Matthew 4:1-11). He offered Jesus worldly things that seemed to give life but could not grant eternal life. We get offered these glamorous things as well.

There are temptations to money, power, control, and reputation. These are at best distractions from our walk of holiness and, in many cases, sinful. In recent history, we've seen the tragic effects of sin—the harm they can do to the sinner and to others. Our baptismal promises begin with a rejection of sin and the glamour of evil.

In a time of fear, we proclaim some bold truths about whose we are and where we are going. We profess that we believe in God the Father, the Creator of all things. We believe in Jesus Christ, who is no stranger to suffering and who, through his death and resurrection, offers us abundant life now and forever. We believe in the Holy Spirit and the fact that, as this Spirit shows us our sins and where we can grow, we can be forgiven and set free.

"

Print your baptismal
promises. . . . Use
them to remind you
who are and where
you are going.

We believe in life everlasting. Our life here on earth isn't the end. It is only the beginning.

We need to go back to the roots of our faith in our Baptism. This moment of history demands it, not simply for the hope that Baptism promises, but for the mission to which that sacrament unites us. Our world needs hope bearers. It needs people who know that there is a God and that God loves us, suffers with us, saves us, and draws us close to himself. People need to be invited into this incredible family. We can do that for them.

Even though we profess our baptismal promises every year at Easter, I propose that this become a weekly occurrence. Print your baptismal promises on a card that you can keep in your wallet or purse, and take two minutes to review them before every Sunday Mass. Don't just read them, but pray them. Recommit yourself to them. Use them to remind you who you are and where you are going. I think this simple prayer will change your experience of Mass.

It all goes back to Baptism, this moment that many of us do not remember but that changed our lives. While we can never be baptized again (once is enough!), we can reengage the grace that we found there. We can recommit to our promises. We can enter into the mission, and we can remember hope.

In Baptism we found hope, because the seed of salvation was given to us. This isn't a maybe. It isn't a "wait and see." It is a promise that, as long as we do not reject that salvation, will come to fulfillment on the day we pass from this life to the next. What we do in between is up to the Holy Spirit and our response.

We can begin now. The final prayer of this book is the renewal of baptismal promises. Don't rush through this. Pray. Let the weight of these commitments fall on you in a glorious way. You were dead, but Baptism brought you to life. These promises are what it means to live in freedom, to live your Baptism and unleash the power of God within you. **After each statement, quietly respond, "I do":**

Do you renounce sin, so as to live in the freedom of the children of God?

Do you renounce the lure of evil, so that sin may have no mastery over you?

Do you renounce Satan, the author and prince of sin?

Do you believe in God, the Father almighty, Creator of heaven and earth?

Do you believe in Jesus Christ, his only Son, our Lord, who was born of the Virgin Mary, suffered death and was buried, rose again from the dead and is seated at the right hand of the Father?

Do you believe in the Holy Spirit, the holy Catholic Church, the communion of saints, the forgiveness of sins, the resurrection of the body, and life everlasting?

Take a moment to offer God a prayer unique to you. Thank God for the gift of Baptism, and ask for grace, abundant life, and hope. Finally, ask for the courage to share this gift with others and live the freedom found in Christ.